UNRAVELLING
Loving my parents through dementia

by Claire Belberg

UNRAVELLING: LOVING MY PARENTS THROUGH DEMENTIA

© 2024 Claire Belberg. All rights reserved. No part of this book may be copied, reproduced or transmitted by any means without prior permission of the author, except in the case of brief quotations embodied in review articles.

Cataloguing-in-Publication entry is available from the National Library of Australia
http:/catalogue.nla.gov.au/.

This edition first published in Hackham, South Australia by Immortalise via Ingram Spark in September 2024.

www.immortalise.com.au

ISBN	print	978-0-6459991-8-1
	ebook	978-0-6459991-9-8

Typesetting by Ben Morton

Cover by Preloaded Design

To Lee

I don't know how I could have made it through

without you

With gratitude to my parents

whose love was evident through all our shared years.

Contents

Meet my family 1
This book: 5
Glimpsing ahead 7
A new normal 9
The first crisis 15
Home alone 23
Endings and beginnings 31
The pandemic effect 41
Their first year in care 47
Rhythms of winter 55
Second crisis 63
Looking back 71
Final words 79
Post-script 81
Acknowledgements 83
Resources 85

Meet my family

Both my parents live with dementia. My father's father had dementia, and his father before him. My mother's mother had dementia and her mother before her.

With all that family history, you might imagine that stories were told and wisdom learned. But dementia has, unfortunately, been a topic of fear and shame for a long time. My parents were children when they saw the effects of dementia on their grandparents. Mum and Dad were on a different continent when their parents were elderly. They did not see firsthand the impact of dementia on them and the family members who cared for them. We never talked about it in my childhood home except when they made mention in passing of a grandparent who was 'odd' or 'difficult'.

I come from a migration-rich family. My great-grandparents moved countries, as did their children, and most of their grandchildren. My first cousins live on five different continents. None of them lived in Australia when I was growing up.

I am the only living child of my parents. Their worst trauma was my brother's suicide at the age of 23. Now that my parents need care, there is no one else in the family but me to provide it. Many of my parents' friends have already died. The remaining friends we knew as I grew up are dealing with their own personal and family issues. Such is life for many in their eighties and nineties. I am exceedingly grateful to the people who provide a home and daily care for my parents.

Around the time we began to see the symptoms of dementia in my parents, my beloved father-in-law died. That signalled the beginning of a journey of lament as I navigated my growing care role for my parents while our youngest child was still at home. Our children also faced the loss of relationship with their grandparents. Unlike me, they had grown up with their grandparents as an integral part of their lives. The changes cut deeply. Grief and loss have been a large part of the last five years of my life, and have impacted my physical and mental health, which adds further complexities.

Like all the other families of the estimated 472,000 Australians living with dementia in Australia in 2021, our family has a unique story. It can help to tell these stories. When I meet people of my generation, telling my story touches issues they are also facing or fearing.

By giving you glimpses into my experience of loving people with dementia, my hope is that you will also find the story comforting as you journey uniquely with your loved ones. You may, however, find it painfully confronting. I am sorry if that's the case.

Books can be a starting point for conversation, so if you have something you want to say in response to the thoughts in this little book, you are welcome to contact me (bellwriting@gmail.com). I can't provide professional help or advice, but I would be pleased to hear something of your story.

THIS BOOK

Unravelling: Loving my parents through dementia is presented as a combination of prose and poetry. Each chapter (group of poems) is introduced by a section of prose to give context.

Poetry can be thought of as 'word snapshots', small moments when a reader is allowed into the inner sanctum of the poet's mind and heart. This collection is in order of the events as they happened so that it reads like a story, following my emotional journey. You can read it in any order, of course, but the story will make more sense chronologically.

You may find the early poems quite stark, even disturbing, but later there are times of humour, pleasure, quiet joy and calm sadness. In life, when you feel there is nothing but pain and loss, it helps to be reminded that the sun still shines gloriously on autumn leaves, good food still tastes marvellous, and there is kindness, often unexpected, to nourish hope.

If the poems distress you, please consider seeking professional help. There are resources at the back of the book for those wanting further information or support.

Glimpsing ahead

While the journey of caring for someone with dementia might start with frustration, dread and a sense of the surreal, over time the perspective shifts. Before we launch into the hard days of my journey, let me give you a glimpse into the future.

Eyes

I begin to see.
For over three years my eyes
have been darkened
by sorrow,
my heart laden with unwanted change.
On a bend that never straightened,
there was no light at the end.
But now

I can laugh.
I can appreciate small joys.
Change happened, dragging
me with it.
Though the tunnel is not straight
shafts of light pierce the gloom,
my adapted eyes seeing more
than I imagined was there.
Even in a dark place
there's light. You just need
to give your eyes time to adjust.

A NEW NORMAL

The mother I grew up with was a wonderful listener, empathetic and nurturing. One day a few years ago, I realised my mother was not the same any more. Just like that, the difference jumped out at me even though I was seeing her twice a week. It felt surreal. Changes had been happening and we had been adapting, but finally a line was crossed and I understood that we were in new territory. I was out of my depth.

Having crossed that line, I revisited the poem I had written the previous year ('Forecast') and saw how subtle the warning had been. Frontotemporal dementia, unfortunately, is difficult to recognise at first and many relationships may be damaged before a diagnosis is given.

With Dad, it was a slow slide. We suspected it was happening, but apart from helping out with banking and putting legal papers in order, I did not know what else could be done.

It might help, at this point, to provide some definitions. 'Dementia' is an umbrella term for a range of neurological diseases that cause cognitive decline. It is not synonymous with old age – although the brain changes with old age, this is not the cause of dementia. Most people are aware of Alzheimer's Disease, as this is the most commonly diagnosed cause of cognitive impairment in the elderly. As a result, much more information exists about it than other forms of dementia. Other forms include Frontotemporal Degeneration, Lewy Body dementia, and vascular dementias. It's not uncommon to experience more than one form of dementia.

Dementia does not, in fact, only occur in the elderly, although it is most common in that age group. Younger Onset Dementia can begin to affect people in their thirties, and Frontotemporal Degeneration typically starts to show in the fifties and sixties.

Only certain types of dementia are known to be genetically related, but there is more research needed to understand this fully.

Early in my understanding of my parents' cognitive decline, I recognised that the primary gift we give to those who live with dementia is to remember who they were and who, I believe, they still are deep within.

Forecast

I've lost my parents.
They haven't died.
As far as I know, they don't have dementia. *
They live in their own home three minutes from
  mine.
They don't suffer medical crisis or financial straits.
But they're gone.
I can't find the people they once were.

If Mum were a favourite soft toy, I'd think the dog
  they don't have had teased out all her stuffing.
Dad would be the wind-up dune buggy with the
  broken cogs.
No energy, no expectation.
They are contained in their overheated rooms of
  tinted window and unchanging routine.

Today a storm is expected,
something spectacular from somewhere else.
But on my regular Wednesday visit
(make an omelette for Mum's lunch and mine,
help with puzzles,
read the recipes Mum saved from the newspaper)

they are ignorant of the coming storm
and expect their small world to remain dry and
windless.

* This was written before we understood that the changes we were seeing were, in fact, caused by dementia.

Mother's Day

We give cards
chosen, maybe handmade,
thoughtfully worded.

I outdid tradition this time:
I added beautiful blue Dutch irises
and white carnations in a cloud of gypsophila.

Then there was the turkey roast
followed by orange-with-fruit jelly
and all the family there to celebrate.

'Where are my other presents?'
'There's no room for the flowers there.'

No joy light in her eyes for the beauty,
no words of pleasure in the meal eaten voraciously,
no curiosity in conversation.

Mother's Day was always a pleasant low-key event
on our family calendar.
Trying to make it 'more special' fell flat. So did I.

Her story

The veil descends
and vandalism of the divine image
grows bolder.

'I am a person, not just your mother,'
she etched into my young mind.
I hold out fiercely for her personhood
as irrationality and diminished capacity
hang like soiled, over-sized garments
on her wizened frame.

I pursue memory
to draw again the creative, courageous woman
who taught me that every life matters,
that every story is worth listening to.

She consumes stories, reading ceaselessly
while her own story and mine
no longer hold her attention.
But I tell them anyway,
determined to keep her image
on the retina of my mind's eye.

The first crisis

My parents had said all my adult life that they didn't want to move out of their house before they died. Having to go against this deep desire was horribly difficult. Finding a way to achieve it seemed impossible.

Dementia often impacts a person's insight, so although it was clear to others that they would need to move at some point, my parents were not capable of exploring their options. The family recognised that any impetus for change would have to come from outside: a crisis. I have since spoken with others who found themselves in the same tragic dilemma.

The crisis happened on Easter Sunday. We discovered Mum had been lying on the floor of their bedroom for more than twelve hours, and insisted on sending her to hospital. It was her second emergency stay in a month; this time the doctors refused to send her home. The aged care facility I had chosen in advance found her a room, and she has lived there ever since.

My mother has not told me how she felt about never seeing her home again. Her dementia has robbed her of the ability to be conscious of her own emotions and to express them verbally. But I live with the memory of how she would once have felt about it, and I hope her lack of insight shields her from the pain of her loss.

My father, having been Mum's carer for several years, could not let go of the role. She became his fixation, and the care home staff quickly got to know him as he spent most of each day with her.

As a way to help the staff learn the kind of person Mum is, her former interests and talents, I made a poster for her wall that included the last seven lines of the poem 'Homeland', surrounded by photographs to provide examples of each phrase.

'Show ride' was shared with fellow participants at a workshop run by Dementia Australia later that year.

Show ride

The scariest show rides of my youth
were the roller coaster, and the Gravitron
which looped the two-seater car,
spinning on its own axis,
around the other gyrating cars
full of screaming, vomiting kids.
I never tried the roller coaster.

I didn't expect I'd be on those rides
endlessly, simultaneously, without choice or payment
– the tickets were inherited –
many long years after I'd worked out that
thrills aren't my thing.

I swing between two spinning cars
– Mum, Dad –
and for days we coast comfortably,
settling into new dynamics, slowly circling.
Jerked sideways without warning,
the spin accelerates.
We hurtle downhill towards an inevitable crash
saved at the last moment to launch skywards
looping, looping
the ground
the sky
the jolt to the stomach

the reel of the mind.

When will it slow?
Where will it take me next?
Will there be anything left inside me when it's done?

Homeland

We see a wide-eyed, white-haired woman
gaunt with weight loss,
bones overlarge in her frame,
life limited to a chair and a novel.

But underneath that tissue-thin skin
has long dwelt a one-woman guerrilla band
   determined
to keep hold of her homeland.

***

The enemy was insidious, creeping upon your joints
   from an early age,
making pain your unwanted comrade.
But you'd always lived in a troubled landscape
from the wilds of the Canadian Rockies
to the heartland of Natal,
family torn and always moving, separating,
dividing across three continents.

There were good years, though shadow-hatched,
years of mothering and crafts
blossoming into visual arts and fervent community-
   building.

Our walls give testament to your vision
and your grandchildren are sculpted by your generous
   free spirit.

Two ambushes shifted your battle onto frighteningly
   shaky ground
      –   the loss of your son
and a tendon injury leading to permanent disability –
traumas that pared you back to the essence
and the primal fight for survival.

And you survived
scarred, minus the use of limbs you miss every day,
and now buried
under the rubble of a deconstructing mind.

***

The battle to hold your homeland enters a new phase
as what you dreaded comes upon you:
a forced move from your only true home.
But, Mum, you take your homeland with you.
In spite of every grief, your war is not lost
for you will always be you
whether it's visible or not –
gift-giving
tree-planting
clay-moulding
heart-listening

image-forming
word-wrangling
you.

The crossword

Always a structure in our family life
the crossword has become the safety grid
we stand on whenever we visit you,
to keep us from plunging into the tunnels below.

You were always in control of the pen, the clues,
filling the boxes faster than you could ask the
    questions,
seeking our involvement only when you wanted
the power of the Internet's mighty memory.

Now we read the clues aloud,
hold off telling the obvious answers to give you time,
schedule the order of questions to maximise your
    dwindling success.
Some days you still surprise us with archaic words
    we've never heard,
swift memory alighting upon your mind though the
    easy words are flighty.

More often we fill in the blanks you leave,
work our way through the Quick, the Two Speed
and as much of the Big One as it takes
before your dinner arrives,
and our reprieve.

Home alone

Without Mum at home with him, Dad was lost. He had already been struggling to discern night from day, and now that he wanted to visit Mum all the time, he would drive to her new home whenever he had the urge. The staff became accustomed to him banging on the locked door in the night, and kindly let him in. He would walk into Mum's room while they tried to reason with him that she was sleeping, and offered him cups of tea and a place to rest while he waited. They could never convince him.

On many occasions while driving to see Mum, Dad lost his bearings. He would stop to ask for help. Some kind folk would look up the address, drive there and have him follow them. Some called the home a little later to check that he had found it.

As much as Dad was attached to his home, he did not like spending time there without Mum. The memories were good (he conveniently forgot all the sad memories) but the life had gone out of it. He was forgetting how to use the equipment: computer, microwave, and remote control units.

Occasionally I would find the front door wide open when he was visiting Mum or shopping.

It became apparent that he was not eating well, so I put meals in his freezer. When he ran out of bottled gas for the stove, I asked the gas company to disconnect it. He couldn't manage more than heating food in the microwave by then, so I'm not sure he noticed.

Dad didn't throw anything away, and would arrange all the mail in neat piles on the dining table. That was useful, as I could easily see when there were bills to pay and letters to attend to. He could read the words but would not understand the meaning, and would be anxious about anything that related to money. It was distressing to see how everyday living was already beyond Dad's capacity. He needed my help every day; I was glad we lived nearby.

I searched out ways to get some assistance but Dad was reluctant to allow anyone outside the family to help. The exception was the weekly cleaner — she was a godsend, so much more than a cleaner. She listened to Dad's repeated stories with genuine interest and found ways to encourage him and make life a little easier for him.

Six months after Mum moved, Dad's driving ability was assessed. It was a thorough process and I was present for all but the practical test. Dad failed convincingly.

This was a huge blow to his independence, his pride, and his pleasure. He had already given up golf, art painting, reading, and doing puzzles. His life revolved around seeing Mum, walking around the garden, and driving.

I arranged transport for every morning of the week, called him in the evening to remind him, called him in the morning to make sure he remembered and was ready. There were notes on the fridge. It was the same routine every day. But it didn't work because of Dad's inability to read the time.

Dad's agitation in this period became unbearable for our daughter, who used the lower storey of the house as an office. She told me he would bang doors, walk around the house calling for me because he'd 'heard' my voice and thought I was teasing him by not showing myself, and then she'd find him at the roadside trying to wave down cars. Just recently a neighbour reminisced about how she had brought Dad down from the road numerous times. Dad's invisible safety net, formed by the kindness of neighbours and strangers, has been a surprising theme of these risky years.

New housemate

Dad didn't do 'dropping in'.
He liked his own space
and he never wanted to 'impose'.

Loneliness chased him out of his house.

He would arrive at ours unannounced,
accept a cup of tea and a biscuit,
and talk.

At his house, loneliness insisted on silence.

The day he couldn't start the car,
he walked to us. He lost his way.

When the off-duty policeman offered him a lift,
he accepted. He forgot our address.

When he told us the story,
he was not embarrassed.
He just laughed,
happy, oh so happy to leave loneliness at home
for an afternoon.

How many times?

Time is Dad's enduring conundrum.
When he's ready and the taxi driver hasn't come
though the long hand is on the 12,
he cannot solve the riddle.

How many hours have I spent
explaining how to read his watch,
noting both hands?
How many nights has he left increasingly desperate messages
cursing faithless cabbies?
How many mornings do my calls ring out
because he'd arrived at the aged care home
to visit Mum at 5am?

I'm trying not to count anything.
Just explain it, simplify it, diagram it
as endlessly as he stumbles.

'How do you stay so calm? How can you keep on doing it?'
my eye-rolling husband asks admiringly,
and, honestly, I don't recognise myself in this.
I guess love is fruiting patience.

Car memoirs

Dad's car was an extension of himself.

As a boy, he was the designated fixer of the family car.
He told boundless stories of the dodgy vehicles
he'd owned in his penniless days,
anecdotes that elicited gasps and bursts of laughter.
Oddly, I never saw him work on our family cars.

But driving was another matter. The car was his freedom.
Stories of road trips through south-eastern Africa
were matched by our holidays driving and camping in Australia.
Sunday drives, just exploring, were his indulgence.

After Mum moved, he liked to find new roads near her home.
He usually got lost but he wasn't fazed.
Mysterious dents began to appear.
They were always someone else's fault,
or even the car's. It just moved by itself.

Never having had a road accident,
he believed implicitly in his driving ability,
and no driving tests could prove to him otherwise.

I kept the car at my place to keep him honest.
He ranted, he agitated, he grieved in the only way he could
all the losses brought by being stripped of that little card.

Later, he would watch the care home car park
trying to work out why all those cars were 'just left there'.
Every car needed him to do something,
something he couldn't remember.

Held

I had the strangest notion:
beyond the morning and evening calls,
the waiting until each day's program has proceeded
   without drama,
the appointments and the endless repetition,
there was no life.

This is it, my life: each day the same,
each day I am the one certainty in my father's
   spinning world
connected by the insentient thread of phone
   communications,
while I float away from my other selves.
Life with my husband, my children,
my faith community, my friends
is mere chimera.

It turns out to be a mirror image:
Someone listens patiently to my endless repetition,
provides an invisible safety net for me,
anchors me in a more solid, more dependable reality
and the fragile thread I cannot always sense
holds me.
Though I float, losing my footing even as my father
   does,
I am not lost.

Endings and beginnings

A few weeks after Dad lost his licence, we spoke to him about the necessity for moving into the home with Mum. We focused on his needs: to be close to Mum, for better food, for help with his medications, and for company and activities he could manage. He was adamant that he would not move, and I backed down. I hated to push him to do something so against his grain. The impossibility of the situation weighed on me so heavily, I needed help to keep going. But I determined to keep him in his home as long as I could.

Three months later, after I had kept a chart to track his behaviours so I could be objective about the decision, I reached the point where I knew he had to move. This time I told him it was as much for my mental health as for his needs. I was astonished that he capitulated without a fight. He often expressed his gratitude for all I did for him. On this day, he understood that his needs were overwhelming me, and his father's heart asserted itself. He accepted what he dreaded for my sake. I have never felt his love so strongly.

He complied with viewing the room that was available, and we set a date for the move a few days later. Each time he visited Mum, he visited his room and we added his favourite paintings to its walls.

I had an extraordinary conversation with him when he asked what would happen to their house. I didn't want this talk. I didn't expect him to understand. I just had to do it because that's what respect looks like. It was the only home they had ever owned; most of their marriage and all of my childhood were spent there. He asked sensible questions in response to my information. He had the sustained cognitive clarity of two years earlier. He never remembered that conversation but it gave me courage to press on.

From here on, the visits the family made were with both of my parents, a much easier arrangement than trying to see them independently. That's not to say they were easy.

Home with a view

The view from our house
never failed to delight. Guests
visiting for the first time would
enter the lounge and continue forward,
drawn instinctively to the wall of windows,
exclaiming, 'Now that's a view!'
Facing east towards a deep gully between
smooth rounded hills of green grass,
across a wide valley which had
for over 100 years centred its activity
on growing apples and pears,
and all the tall trees that had been planted
in the urban sprawl of the seventies.
Not least the oak, eucalypts and pine
planted by my mother a decade earlier than that,
the bones of the garden she designed and grew
from a grass-matted hillside.

This view.
Sheeting rain in winter like a waterfall surrounding.
Fogs that flattened the hills to an imaginary plain,
   breath
to draw guilty swirls on the mist-painted glass.
Late afternoon golden glow on the other-side hills,
sunset rose flaunting the dusk hidden by the hill at
   our backs.

Cockatoos soaring the heat-warped azure skies before us,
rosellas and honeyeaters in the oak that reaches to the balcony,
sparrows and starlings tapping at the top windows.
Koala recumbent in the fork of the spotted gum
directly in front of us, our private viewing station.

They never meant to leave this view,
counting only on a final exit in a box.
The one place Mum put down her own roots;
the home of Dad's design and build.
The last place they knew their son,
and the three-generation joys of grandchildren
staying for the summer.

When he knew no difference between night and day,
Dad would draw the curtains open,
gaze at the view, trying to use
the silhouettes of the hills to tell the time.
In those last weeks living there
in the loneliness and confusion,
the view was his comfort. He
would breathe deeply then
know joy, the wonder that never faded.

He moved!

It all happened so quickly.
One day I knew it was time.
I told him,
I spoke to the aged care home,
and suddenly he lived there.

Every day I had steeled myself
to manage the inevitable push back
that never came.

It was hilariously anti-climactic
the day his new life began,
as he'd taken himself there by taxi
at 3am
and was found by the morning shift
sitting in his armchair
waiting for a mattress to be added to the bedframe.

Is he happy? I don't know.
I don't ask.
and, really, I don't care.
He's safe, he's fed, he washes,
he participates and he can see his wife
whenever he wants to,
and he doesn't have to wait any more
for the 'damn taxi' to come.

Conjuring happiness

He liked the room from the start,
as rooms go,
if he had to have only one room instead
of a cold, lonely, memory-weighted house
with a view he never tired of in 58 years.

He liked that it had a sliding door to the long
　courtyard,
a second exit that wasn't a hall,
a way of escape from the anonymity of doors
that made his space just like everyone else's.

He liked the new reclining armchair
that was unlike anything he had owned before,
but he only sat in the familiar chair
brought from home, unless I sat in it first.

It wasn't home. It was nice for people
who liked that sort of place.
(Not their sort of people. They were never like that.)
It was okay but it wasn't them.
(Could they go home?)

Time and dementia
have worked some dark magic,
and sheer repetition has conjured familiarity

even as significant memories lose their shapes
and recent past blurs with early years.

He tells me it's a good place,
he's comfortable and
they look after him well,
plenty of good food,
and, really, it's just the distance
between his room and hers that palls.
And the riverside gums he can see over the roof
on the other side of the courtyard –
magnificent.
Walking under them daily
as a guided group activity
brings him joy. It's good.

And I'm glad he's feeling more at home
but I feel like we all did a number on him.
Perhaps it is good.

Visits

Presence is what they crave,
physical nearness.
We cannot satisfy it.
Even when I visited every day
the moment of parting would come:
'Must you go?'
Now it's a weekly visit
and, of course,
it is not enough.
'I missed you.'
'Could you see us more often,
just a bit more often?'

No.
I don't say it, of course.
I don't tell them how my days
and my consciousness
revolved so totally around them
for two years
that I almost broke.
I don't let on how the visits
sap me, depress me
by the evident decline after each seven days,
or how we labour to make the visits
pleasant and
meaningful and

stimulating,
how exhausting it is
to dovetail crosswords for one
with repetitive interruptions by the other
in a darkened room
and the amplified sounds from the corridor
(and him hard of hearing
and her with breathless voice).

It's not really about what we do
or what is said
so much as being there.
That is hard enough.

THE PANDEMIC EFFECT

The timing of Dad's move into care was perfect. We didn't know that only three weeks later the world would begin to shut down against a pandemic. Covid-19 changed everything. As Dad wanted more than anything to be with Mum each day, suffering the lockdowns with her was far less distressing than otherwise.

I expected to have months to settle Dad into a life he had dreaded, at the same time as continuing to give Mum quality attention. Instead, I got sick and couldn't visit at all, and then we were all in lockdown. This became a much-needed respite for me. Dad, as it turned out, didn't need me to help him settle.

After a while the care home developed ways for us to stay in touch with our loved ones when visiting wasn't allowed. There were iPads for face-to-face calls, then we had 'window visits', and later we could use a special room they set up for screen-separated visits inside. My parents found the iPad confusing (video calls with their granddaughter overseas had been tricky for some time), and Mum doesn't do conversation any more. I organised delivery of the occasional parcel of flowers and favourite snacks, but there was no way around the reality that lockdowns caused painful separation.

Anxious

Mere weeks ago I was
burdened
with the care of my father,
chased day and night
by the avalanche of his needs. Now
I worry
that I cannot see or talk with him,
separated
as I am from my parents in lockdown.
Thankful
they are together, provided for,
safer than in their own home,
I wonder
if – when – I will see them again,
for containment works both ways
and their safe home could become an incubator.
God forbid.

It comes to this

I signed the paper when
it was obvious that someone
should play backstop.
I committed to make future decisions
as if I were they.
I have made many.

Today I wrestle with one
no one wants to make,
the decision that could precipitate their deaths.

They have Covid-19.
It came the previous week with a visitor.
First one, then nineteen,
now over a third of the residents are infected.
Most are vaccinated.
Most have dementia.

And I'm told it's my decision
whether my parents go to hospital
once oxygen is required.

The knee-jerk says, 'Of course!'
But there's Mum's 'no resus' order...
But there's Dad's primary motive to be with Mum...
But there's dementia's demand for familiarity...

Would I sacrifice these
simply to prolong life?

Am I God, that I should choose?
If I were, I would know the unknowable:
will they survive?
will they suffer long-lasting complications?
will they suffer more
if I decide to say, 'No'?

Their first year in care

Mum and Dad survived their brush with Covid-19 without any physical effects, though the isolation took its toll. Their first year or so of residential care saw a variety of other challenges too. I had learned how to work with the residential care staff for Mum, but Dad's needs and responses were so different that the learning curve began again when he moved in, complicated by the ever-changing landscapes of dementia and the pandemic.

The staff were happy to support small family celebrations (except during the heights of the pandemic). They provided a tea trolley, commercial biscuits and kitchen-made cake for us. Trying to make sure the resident was ready and appropriately dressed was a little harder.

It was at group events that my mother's dementia became most obvious, like an experienced actor forgetting their lines. As interests and activity contracted, buying gifts became more difficult. In the year after Dad moved, we celebrated their birthdays, their 60th wedding anniversary and Christmas.

Oddly, laundry turned out to be a frequent issue when they moved. Even properly labelled garments went missing, never to be seen again, especially newly purchased items. Whatever it is that eats socks in the environment of the family home is a lot hungrier in a residential institution!

During this year, in addition to calling on various health services available at the home, Dad had two short, distressing hospital stays for surgery. Every new challenge triggered hard questions in me.

Mum and Dad had much to learn, too, in their first years of living in a residential institution, as they experienced reduced control over their environment. I found it difficult to be their advocate when I could not be sure what was actually happening and how they felt about it. So much of my peace of mind depends on trusting that they are being cared for well.

Autumn birthday

Ho hum, she's turning 89.
Last year I bought a fancy cake
with flower crown,
and an autumn green jumper.
The flowers were appreciated.

You get used to dementia
like a familiar jumper wearing at the cuffs,
and get on with your days.
The gradual autumnal
decline of light and warmth
is almost cosy, a gentle rhythm.

The birthday returns to me sadness,
reawakening the sharp sense
of this between-life.
What can I give to bring joy
to a woman who cannot?
There are flowers, of course.
Always flowers, thank God.

Buried alive

Watching someone you love develop dementia
is like standing by as they get buried alive
and being unable to intervene.

First it was her feet unable to carry her to the kitchen
    or the studio,
then her hands too shaky to hold pencil or brush,
her voice became devoid of will and projection,
and her desire to give, to encourage, to celebrate was
    punctured
until only a residual wisp remains.

Damned frontal lobe degeneration,
undoing the layers of personality
built over a lifetime, revealing…
something other than the core of the woman,
some half-formed element still unravelling.

Conversation with the doctor

'What was your profession?'
the urologist asks personably.
Same as the doctor's now-dead father, it turns out.
'Commercial or domestic?'
Dad is launched,
thirty plus years of local architecture
overshadowed by the focus
on his best three:
Kariba on the Zambezi River.

Turning to the business at hand,
the doctor moves on to recent events:
symptoms, tests,
medical history, plans.
He seeks Dad's input,
probing body memories,
getting no response.
Sometimes Dad comments:
'I wasn't the only one, of course,
there were three of us in charge.'
The doctor and I continue
to exchange information.

'We answered to Head Office

in Salisbury.'
'I'm listening with half an ear,'
the doctor kindly notes
while entering data on his computer.
'It all came good,' Dad adds,
'nothing wrong with me at all.'

And the doctor, trying to join
the random dots,
says, 'I don't think it was your job
on the Zambezi River
that caused your bladder polyps.'

The visit ends with Dad telling the doctor
the one about the monkey and the bananas.

'He didn't do much, did he?'
Dad summarises the following day.
'He showed us pictures of your bladder.'
'I didn't see any pictures!'
'Well, Dad, I have forty minutes
of information downloaded
to my brain.
And you're scheduled for surgery.
He did enough.'

The photo album

It was a beautiful album,
if I say so myself:
the people she loved,
decorated and designed,
ordered chronologically.

It was a risk calculated
to give her the best chance of
recognition through dim eyes
and dirty glasses.
It was vulnerable to dribble and sticky fingers.

Four weeks after Christmas
the album lies denuded
of every decorative element.
The disorder of the photographs
reflects her cognitive confusion
and photos are mysteriously torn.
I try an on-the-spot restoration,
some effort to echo the original design.

The following week she mentions the album
in a rare comment:
'You made a real mess of it.'
I wait until we are on our way home
to laugh aloud.

Rhythms of winter

Old age has been called the winter of life. It can be a difficult season, and dementia (and other diseases) adds to the challenge. But like winter, if we can move through the discomfort and limitations it imposes, there are quiet joys that help us to appreciate the deeper things of life, the things and people that matter most. Once my parents and I had adjusted to the new shape of their lives, and my 'unravelling' slowed, I found laughter and joy beginning to poke out like tiny shoots. I began to look past the sadness and uncertainty that are still part of my world, to see beauty and enjoy small pleasures as I spent time with Mum and Dad.

The rhythms of this season are about making the most of what we still have. I have adapted somewhat to the changes happening to my parents and our relationship. Sadness and joy can now live side by side in me, an ebb and flow that is almost as regular as gentle waves on the beach.

Golf

'He's been on my back
ever since I moved here',
Dad claims earnestly
and with surprising consistency.
'He wants me to play a round of golf.
I'd like that.'

It started with a form letter
from the local MP
welcoming him to the electorate.
None of the content
made any sense to Dad
but somehow he read into it
that this fellow had invited him to play.
No evidence to the contrary
dislodged the notion.

He seriously believes
he is capable, that his ninety-year-old body
which has walked no more than a kilometre
at any time in the last year
can cover a golf course.
Two games of lawn bowls
nearly knocked him out,
literally, eighteen months ago.

Okay, I say.
Forget the politician.
I'll take you out for nine holes.

I don't think he'll make it
but how can it hurt
to be out in the air on the greens,
to swing a club
and enact the memories
of sixty plus years of golf?
And if he manages,
if it brings him joy,
I might just call that MP
to thank him.

Now is what matters – his 90th

I remember.
A windy, warm autumn day
and a covered outdoor area.
Family gathered, decorations
created with loving labour,
thoughtful gifts and
a platter of savoury nibbles.

Greetings from his sisters overseas
and a big cake from the care home kitchen
all proclaimed the grand age.
He couldn't comprehend it
but he enjoyed the minor fuss.
He could still rise to occasion.

It was a small event
but that's how he liked it.
The cake was excellent,
and the afternoon lovely.
It was just about perfect.

What difference would it have made
if he later remembered
the party or his age?
We're all learning to make the most of now.

The outing

One winter afternoon, sun
glazing wet leaves
under a lowering sky,
I take Dad through streets
thick with after-school traffic.
He gazes with fascination,
noting buildings and scapes
with an architect's eye.
We hasten on foot beside
an iconic, Old Adelaide road
and cross –
   a car plays chicken
   as Dad's 'fast' pace continues unaltered
   to the far side
– and we enter a genteel house
cum professional rooms.

An hour later, sunset nearing,
we retrace our steps, less rushed.
I repeat the doctor's words:
probably cancer
surgery booked for three weeks hence.
Our return journey –
   the daylight dimmed,
   street lamps and buildings
   lit like near stars,

    traffic pressed towards home
– is coloured by Dad's wonder,
this time for the 'new' scenes
remodelled by night.

Waiting for his reserved dinner
to be retrieved by care staff,
Dad glows.
As I leave, he repeats:
'Thank you for the outing.'

Second crisis

The possibility of cancer threatens both my parents at this point, but further tests and treatments are not planned. The doctors and I recognise that my parents are on the downhill run, but there's no knowing time frames. All seemed to be drifting and uncertain until Dad took a sudden turn for the worse, and the end seems more real now. But still we live with uncertainty as he has more good days than bad; I am grateful it's that way.

On the whole, I managed this sudden change without the intense anxiety and distress of the first crisis. But the shock of change is still real, and the uncertainty of how it will progress makes it difficult to come to terms with.

The phone rings

'I'm calling about your father – don't worry, he's
   okay...'
It's several times most weeks now,
a call from the aged care home
about Mum's skin breaking down
or Dad falling.

I asked Mum if she is worried when she falls head
   first
out of bed.
'Very frightened,' she replied, which is something
from the woman whose standard answer to 'How are
   you?'
is 'Fine. I'm always fine.'

Remarkably neither has broken a bone in their
   frequent falls
and even bruises are rare. We have called the
   ambulance
but Dad recovered quickly with little memory of the
   events.
Which is better than anger or agitation.

He's changed so much in only six months
and our ability to connect meaningfully is limited
to hugs and lollies. Last week he seemed oblivious

to our visit, wandering out of Mum's room and not
   returning,
not even realising when we said goodbye to him at
   the lunch table
that we were there to see him also, just like
every other week in the last three years.

So the phone rings, and I recognise the number.
Will this be the call that says she's not fine anymore
or he's gone, no longer wandering? And part of me

hopes those calls come soon
because it's no fun for them
and it's so hard to see the inevitable
stretch out like
elastic about to
snap.

Unexpected

Not long ago Dad looked like he would last
forever. Then his walk became a shuffle.
His mind was affected long before his body
and the mismatch bothered me. Now he has caught
up with himself, but it's no better after all.

So far he's stayed in bed a week and counting,
as Alzheimer's takes its bleak and weary toll.
'Unless he starts to drink,' the doctor says,
'he only has two weeks at most.' Mere weeks
when not so long ago we thought in years.

And I had wished the end would happen sooner.
Guilt shimmers at the corner of my eye
but I don't look. My prayer has always been
both longing and relinquishment. It's not
my fault if longing hits the winning mark.

I try to salvage hope: he may yet rise,
start drinking, eating, sitting up. But I'll
practice for the end in sight though blurred:
I plan the funeral, trying to picture life
without my father, while he hovers at the edge.

The jacket

Dad's dress sense expressed his professional self.
Collared shirts, cuffs just emerging from the sleeves.
Tailored-style trousers with a good centred crease.
Black leather pull-on shoes, matching socks.
Neatly folded handkerchief always at hand.
No track suits or sneakers unless he was exercising.
No t-shirts, hoodies, ugg boots.
He wasn't a casual kind of guy.

Dad didn't take many clothes into care,
and he wore the same every day by preference.
The jacket was woollen, a well-shaped tweed-style
   garment.
I rarely convinced him to remove it in summer.
It became his personality signature.

'My jacket doesn't fit any more,' he said one day,
showing short sleeves with the lining protruding.
It was tight on him, misshapen.
Apparently a new starter in the laundry knew nothing
about fabrics. The usual launderer assured me
she had taken special care with it.
She knew a quality garment when she saw one.
Lesson learned: don't leave your parents with
   clothing
that can't be tumble-dried.

He continued to wear it. I sought a new one,
 unsuccessfully.
Posters appeared in Dad's room:
'Do not send the jacket to the laundry.'
The posters distress Dad still. He imagines
all sorts of rules from 'the people at the top'.
He can never remember my explanations.

The state of the jacket, however,
is no longer a problem
because now Dad wears trackies, pyjamas, odd shoes.
If he gets out of bed at all.

Leaving

We leave Dad with music playing,
digitised copies of his favourite vinyls.
He lives in bed these days,
and though mention of Mum sparks some memory,
he shows no interest in seeing her.
If nothing else, this is the sign that he's turned a corner
into another dark dementia alley.
Yet he's cheerful enough, and glad to see me.

When I leave, I say, 'I love you, Dad,'
and today his response was 'I love you too'.
I guess no one else says that to him, and so
I still receive the daughter privilege,
even if he doesn't understand the connection.

Staff coax him to get out of bed, sit in his chair,
go for a walk. There's no known bodily reason
why he won't. Another clue to the changed state of his brain.
But nothing has changed for me.
I still find ways to love, to comfort,
communicate with the attentive staff,
do my weeping in poetry and prayer.
And start to plan for the day he leaves us.

Looking back

There is a luxury to being able to look back from a vantage point gained through pain, a vista that is difficult to appreciate during stressful or traumatic events. Then the memories of happier times seemed to be shadowed by current grief. If earlier joys were remembered, they seemed insignificant.

Now that I am not overwhelmed by that pain and grief, I remember. As I prepare (in advance) for eulogies and this book, I find the earlier memories coming forward and some pleasure in that. Grief can paint bittersweet on good memories, but sometimes I actually laugh aloud and enjoy the blessing without complication.

Some of the poems from that vantage point have already appeared in this collection. Here are four more.

Her day in the sun – Mum's 90th

Once again we run the gauntlet of celebrating with
  Mum,
but this time we're all better placed for success.
We come to the home with our party picnic,

spread ourselves out in the courtyard, where the May
  sun
is so unexpectedly warm, I fear Mum will burn.
The shade of the gazebo gathers our four generation
  family

as we swirl like the tide, my mother and grandson
  passive
like rocks to our constant party motion: feeding
  them,
chatting, a flow that renders their limits irrelevant

in the opening of gifts and the pouring of tea,
and the snap of the camera etching in memory
the first and possibly only time with all of us
together.

Proud

They gave her back to me,
Mum's friends,
most of them estranged,
divided from her by dementia
and her apparent lack of interest.

They tell me,
each one with some ambivalence,
that Mum was always direct,
ready to declare a wrong that needed righting.
She spoke out of turn,
ruffling feathers.
She stood in the way of bulldozers
of both kinds, metal and flesh.

On Mother's Day I wrote
quick words on a card of red roses.
The words that flowed surprised me,
rising ripe with honour:
I'm proud to be your daughter.

Not proud of denial
which kept the elephant in the shadows.
Not proud of sharp tongue,
the whip of a sharp mind.
Not proud of refusal

to acknowledge fault and fear,
or to trust to the mercy of friends.

Proud, though, of compassion that risked
the ire of those who preferred order.
Proud of the courage to speak into
the silence that damns conformity.
Proud of the determination to make
something of a self that suffered
the lie she was nothing.

I'm proud to be your daughter.

An old dog

They say you can't,
but life does teach old dogs
new tricks. Witness my dad.

When Mum lost her capacity to stand in the kitchen
to cook or fetch her own snacks,
Dad took over.

At first it was simple meals, Mum directing
from her chair, until she proudly told us
he'd made Lamb Provençal.

He didn't enjoy cooking, or eating that much
really, but he was determined to provide
for his disabled wife. He took up the shopping

from lists she prepared as she planned the meals.
He washed the dishes, and the clothes. Years earlier
  he'd told her
their contract was for him to earn, and her to manage
  the home

but, characteristically, she'd replied, 'What contract?'
And here he was, decades later, crossing boundaries.
He felt inept. I thought he was inspirational.

Talking with Dad

He loves to chat,
though there's nothing new
and even the old,
the stories he loved to tell,
is becoming blurry.

He uses words, and usually
they flow, pattering,
but it's getting harder to know
what he wants them to mean.
The subject is hard to catch,
general words in place of specific
nouns. Lost words echo
lost thoughts, and what's left
is language that struggles to communicate.

I ask questions: do you mean...?
Was that when...?
I draw on my knowledge of his old stories,
his favourite memories,
the family history, to unfurl
the thought that began the words.

The habit of conversation means something
even if ideas are veiled
— togetherness, respect, shared laughter,

affirmation of his being, his unique stamp.
I must remember this.

Final words

The last five years have been sometimes depressing, always challenging, and perspective-changing for me and my family. I have been unravelled as my parents have disappeared before my eyes. I have found myself supported in ways I hadn't expected, and I am learning to find joy in the midst of struggle. I feel I have been oddly enriched by these difficult years.

There are no shortcuts in dealing with the curve balls of life. By acknowledging my pain, accepting help and choosing to love when I just wanted to escape, my struggle has not been wasted. My parents know we love them. I am better equipped to face my own ageing process and I know now that I have a community of support to help me through.

I hope you find these (or other benefits) as you journey this hard, but strangely blessed road with a loved one living with dementia.

Blessings

These days it's easier
to count my blessings
in my parents.
The titanic battle to accept
the devastations of dementia
has been downgraded to a sustainable
sadness like a photographer's backdrop.
I busy myself with daily matters,
harvesting sprigs of joy from ordinary events.
Despite fading memories,
incomprehensible conversations
and incontinence,
I wonder that Dad still knows me.
Their faces light up when we arrive
as, no doubt ours do for our grandbaby.
Dad expressed delight at some new trousers:
'My favourites!'
and Mum, who has developed a sweet tooth,
still knows which chocolate she prefers.
We have our comfortable routines
and as long as they last,
we are blessed.

Post-script

At the time of writing, my parents are still alive. Mum is little changed though she finds the words harder to fetch for the crosswords. She knows us and our names, she knows her two great-grandchildren and whose children they are, but she does not engage with them when they are present. Dad responds to us warmly but we are not confident he could tell you who we are. He lives in bed and, other than the loss of physical strength because of inactivity, he remains well and mostly content, an astonishing comeback from the day we thought he was dying. They both still love to eat chocolate! I am glad to have them still physically present.

October 2023

Acknowledgements

There are more people than I can name who have supported me emotionally and spiritually during these fraught years, from the acquaintances who commiserated and shared their own stories, to those who have touched base with me frequently and intentionally. The same goes for those who support my parents with daily care and respect. To all of you, though unnamed here, please accept my gratitude.

This collection is dedicated to Lee, my spiritual director, who asked each month for more poems, and used them to help me understand and trust: you cried with me, laughed with me and listened closely to my words and my heart. Your faith gave me strength.

Special thanks to my husband, Phil: I am so grateful to you for being calm and caring when I have been overwhelmed and needy, and for being a son to my parents. And gratitude to our adult children for your support of me while you struggled with the loss of the grandparents you had known.

Thank you to Jean, who regularly touched base with me once she lost contact with Mum and Dad. Your ongoing friendship with my parents provided a safe place to pour out my woes to someone who knows my family well.

In the editing of the book and preparation for publication, notable mentions include: Literati – my writing group (especially Valerie Volk, Julia Archer, James Cooper, Catch Tilly, Dimity Knight and Mark Worthing); Tarla Kramer, fellow poet, who gave a thoughtful assessment of the manuscript and suggested improvements; and for health professionals Leah and Wendy (dementia support), Lee and Marie (geriatric care) for reading the manuscript with professional eyes and providing feedback. Your generosity with time and encouragement gave me the courage to create this book.

Resources

When I needed professional help to understand what was happening to my parents, how I could survive the pressure and how to manage their behaviours, I turned to Dementia Australia.

Dementia Australia has branches in every Australian capital city and some country areas. This helpful organisation provides information and support for people living with dementia and their families and caregivers. They provide information sheets, run workshops and seminars, and offer counselling and support groups. **There is also a national helpline (1800 100 500).** Their online resources are available at https://www.dementia.org.au.

They also have libraries that are free to borrow from. Two books I found helpful were:

- *Contented dementia* by Oliver James (based in the UK, very readable, about memory loss dementias)
- *What if it's not Alzheimer's?* edited by Gary Radin and Lisa Radin (based in the US, more academic, about

Frontotemporal Degeneration and some other less common forms of dementia).

Since writing this book, I have learned about Dementia Doulas International, a wonderful recent initiative with a focus on training 'doulas' to walk with the families of those who live with dementia. You can find out more at https://www.dementiadoulas.com.au.

Wendy Hall, the founder and executive director, has written several books on dementia addressing different audiences. The one specifically for families and carers is called *Beyond the darkness of dementia: finding hope when all appears lost*. The book gives voice to those who are so often inadvertently silenced by care systems. Wendy has extensive experience and recognises the needs of families and the ways those working within care systems must change their approach accordingly. It's written with sympathy, respect and practical hope.

Other organisations that may be able to provide less formal support are local dementia and/or carer support groups, faith communities, and local council initiatives within positive ageing networks.

www.ingramcontent.com/pod-product-compliance
Lightning Source LLC
Chambersburg PA
CBHW011151290426
44109CB00025B/2573